# YOUR KNOWLEDGE HAS VALUE

- We will publish your bachelor's and master's thesis, essays and papers

- Your own eBook and book -
  sold worldwide in all relevant shops

- Earn money with each sale

Upload your text at www.GRIN.com
and publish for free

# Strategic Expansion of Beyond Meat's Plant-Based Seafood in the UK. A Sustainable Approach to Market Growth

## SWOT Analysis

Joeleen Kimbell

**Bibliographic information published by the German National Library:**

The German National Library lists this publication in the National Bibliography; detailed bibliographic data are available on the Internet at http://dnb.dnb.de.

ISBN: 9783389092156
This book is also available as an ebook.

© GRIN Publishing GmbH
Trappentreustraße 1
80339 München

Print and binding: Books on Demand GmbH, Norderstedt, Germany
Printed on acid-free paper from responsible sources.

The present work has been carefully prepared. Nevertheless, authors and publishers do not incur liability for the correctness of information, notes, links and advice as well as any printing errors.

GRIN web shop: https://www.grin.com/document/1519223

**Strategic Expansion of Beyond Meat's Plant-Based Seafood in the UK: A Sustainable**

**Approach to Market Growth**

**By**

**Joeleen Kimbell**

**2024**

## Abstract

This strategic proposal looks at the possibility of Beyond Meat growing its plant-based seafood

portfolio in the United Kingdom (UK) market. Beyond Meat, a leading plant-based food firm,

needs to fulfill the growing market need for more environmentally friendly and sustainable food

products as Britons embrace veganism. This proposal evaluates the external market conditions of

the UK using the PESTEL framework, favorable government policies, new business

opportunities in sustainable products, and changing UK consumer trends towards healthier,

environment-friendly living. Moreover, it discusses the usage of plant-based seafood,

technological advancements and environmental impacts of plant-based seafood, and the policy

environment of labeling and marketing of plant-based seafood. A SWOT analysis places Beyond

Meat well concerning traditional rival Quorn Foods and relative newcomer Impossible Foods.

Thus, Beyond Meat can consolidate its position in the UK flexitarian market by using the

company's well-developed brand recognition and retailers' relations.

# Contents

## Introduction

Beyond Meat, founded in California in 2009, is now one of the largest plant-based food companies in the world, committed to reducing environmental impacts associated with animal-based foods (The Strategy Story, 2023). The main objective of Beyond Meat is to develop meat alternatives for those looking to reduce meat consumption while still seeking traditional meat based on the taste and texture expectations of the conventional meat consumer. The company's product portfolio ranges from Beyond Burger and Beyond Sausage to Beyond Meatballs, available in North America, Europe, and parts of Asia.

*Editor's note: Image had to be removed for copyright reasons*

Figure 1:Beyond Meat Products. Source https://www.beyondmeat.com/en-GB/products/

Beyond Meat has continued to increase its exposure to the European market since it first entered the market in 2018, taking full advantage of the growing interest among consumers in the region to switch toward sustainable food and plant-based diets. Beyond Meat distributes its products through retail partnerships with major supermarket chains like Tesco, Sainsbury's, and Carrefour, as well as foodservice partnerships with large brands like McDonald's, KFC, and Pizza Hut. Beyond Meat is also an operationally B2B organization in Europe, with key sales into retail and foodservice.

A fitting scenario exists within the UK market for plant-based alternatives, especially those that focus on environmental sustainability and health benefits by reducing meat consumption. But with growing competition and fluctuating consumer demand, Beyond Meat will need to accelerate the pace. This new line of products, for instance, plant-based seafood, may position Beyond Meat to expand its portfolio and follow emerging consumer trends in sustainable food alternatives, specifically those driven by health-conscious and environmentally sensitive customers.

## Competitor and Market Analysis

### External Market Analysis: PESTEL Framework

The UK plant-based market is dynamic, and conducting a PESTEL analysis helps disclose some factors influencing Beyond Meat's potential for introducing a new product line.

**Political:** The UK government already advocates for environmentally and socially conscious food consumption. The efforts of the UK Climate Change Act, the government's commitment to reduce greenhouse gas emissions, and campaigns started at the national level on plant-based diets are logically reshaping consumer attitudes regarding alternatives to meat. Moreover, post-Brexit tariffs and import costs may shift regulation in a way that can affect the price and profitability of Beyond Meat in the UK market.

**Economic:** The plant-based sector is expected to grow within the UK, especially as awareness of sustainability and health increases. However, inflation and global supply chain disruptions have sparked consumer price sensitivity. Despite this, there has been increased demand for sustainable products for UK-based consumers. Beyond Meat can consider this a key opportunity to be a premium yet environmentally-friendly brand. The plant-based food market in the UK was estimated to be around £1.6 billion in 2022 and is expected to keep growing strongly, driven mostly by increased adoption by flexitarians and vegetarians (USDA Foreign Agricultural Service, 2022).

**Social:** Consumer tastes and preferences for healthier lifestyles and more sustainability are changing exponentially in the UK. Meanwhile, around a quarter of the UK population is now reducing its meat consumption, and events such as "Meat-Free Mondays" and "Veganuary" have raised very widespread awareness of plant-based alternatives (Erangu & Mohankumar, 2021). Indeed, flexitarians-people who consume meat only occasionally but prefer plant-based foods-are a big and fast-growing demographic. It creates a rather fertile ground for Beyond Meat to expand its portfolio into seafood analogs and tap into the health-conscious consumer who wants to reduce their intake of traditional seafood.

**Technology:** The development in food technology allows Beyond Meat to make an offering closest to animal-based meats' taste, texture, and nutritional profile. Plant-based seafood requires flavor and texture engineering through technological advances; here, Beyond Meat can simulate traditional qualities that are more difficult to develop in seafood when compared to land-based meat (Keith, 2024).

**Environmental:** Most UK consumers are now consuming plant-based diets due to environmental concerns. Seafood has received much criticism due to overfishing, habitat loss, and other problems within the sector. Therefore, Plant-based seafood is perceived to have the least environmental impact on all seafood products. Greenhouse Gas Emission: Plant-based meats are estimated to emit as much as 90% fewer greenhouse gases than animal products (Keith, 2024). This will be according to the mission of Beyond Meat and will be a strategic advantage for the brand in promoting its line of eco-friendly products.

**Legal:** The UK has strict labeling laws distinguishing between plant-based and animal-based products. This influences how companies brand and package their products. The UK's legal approach to food labeling is to avoid consumer confusion, so a product like "plant-based seafood" needs to be described appropriately. Of course, adding to the regulatory burden, these requirements also carry transparency that can help engender consumer trust (Keith, 2024).

**Competitor Analysis**

Beyond Meat has tough competitors in the UK plant-based market. Key players include:

**Impossible Foods:** Impossible Foods uses a novel method to create plant-based burgers and meats that have the feel and "bleeding" of fresh meat. The company has not yet developed any significant products in the analog seafood market, which allows Beyond Meat to have the first-mover advantage in the UK plant-based seafood segment (Impossible, 2024).

**Quorn:** This UK-based company offers a portfolio of vegetarian and vegan options, including plant-based fish-like alternatives. Given its built brand reputation, Quorn serves health-oriented consumers and thus demonstrates deep penetration in UK retail. Although Quorn is present in seafood analogs, Beyond Meat can be differentiated using international brand recognition and innovative product technology.

**Nestlé:** Nestlé's Garden Gourmet brand has rapidly expanded its plant-based European portfolio. While highly focused on burgers and sausages, this could be extended to seafood alternatives with the breadth of resources at Nestlé. Beyond Meat will need to focus on the commitment of its brand to quality and sustainability to be a strong competitor against such a diversified player.

Beyond Meat's innovative approach to replicating products positions the brand to attract a certain segment of consumers desiring a taste and texture experience very similar to real meat or seafood. In addition, high-profile food service partnerships, such as those with McDonald's, will help build loyalty and raise the brand's profile within the UK.

## Identification of Sales Opportunity

Beyond Meat's successes in plant-based meat are a good foundation for its move into production related to plant-based seafood alternatives. The decision to engage with plant-based seafood is a response to the growing consumer awareness of sustainability issues related to traditional seafood consumption, including overfishing, plastic pollution, and decreased fish stocks. Research supports this idea that over half of the world's seafood stocks, or about 90%, are fully exploited or overexploited (UNCTAD, 2017). Driving consumer interest in finding alternative, more viable seafood options; on the other hand, with the growing environmental awareness, more and more consumers are inclined to reduce seafood consumption due to the damage it causes to the environment, hence making plant-based seafood a very promising alternative.

### Product: Plant-Based Seafood Line

The proposed product line may comprise plant-based fish fillets, shrimp, and crab cakes. These can be prepared to taste and cook like traditional seafood and can be designed to meet the fast-growing demand for sustainable food alternatives within the UK market.

### Product: Beyond Meat

Beyond Meat will fully unlock its new plant-based seafood line when it can establish a dedicated Seafood Sales Team within the company's European sales division. The Seafood Sales Team would focus exclusively on seafood alternatives in the UK market with current retail and foodservice clients and new accounts interested in seafood substitutes.

### Target Sector and Client

**Retail sector:** Large food retail chains, such as Tesco, Sainsbury's, and Waitrose, would be appropriate distribution channels for Beyond Meat's plant-based seafood line. Tesco, in particular, has shown a very serious commitment to developing and growing its plant-based product line. Thus, targeting Tesco would give Beyond Meat an expansive, mainstream reach of that consumer segment purchasing plant-based products from large retail outlets.

**Food Service Sector:** Beyond Meat and Fish Products could also target highly publicized food service clients focused on sustainability, such as Pret a Manger. Pret a Manger has a very strong market position in the UK and a reputation for making sustainable product choices. Pret's customer base is predominantly young, urban, and eco-conscious; hence, it would be a very apt channel for introducing innovative plant-based seafood options.

## Sales Force Structure Analysis

Beyond Meat has to incorporate the new product line into the existing sales force structure to solidify the launch of the plant-based seafood product line. Beyond Meat's current European sales force, it has a vertical structure that controls retail and food service accounts. This type of structure assists the company in targeting large accounts in every sector to ensure that the big clients have their respective time and customized service.

### Beyond Meat Sales Force Structure and Challenges

Currently, the sales force structure at Beyond Meat consists of two clear divisions: one dealing with retail chains like Tesco and Sainsbury's, amongst others, and another providing its service to food service providers. These include restaurants and fast food chains like McDonald's (Terazono, 2022). Thus, such a sales force structure will enable Beyond Meat to cater to each client's needs effectively. However, offering a new plant-based seafood line has raised some special needs for knowledge and strategic focus since plant-based seafood is a relatively new category with peculiar consumer expectations. Therefore, the existing setup may not capture all the special market dynamics and technical issues that will come into play in marketing seafood alternatives.

**Sales Roles and Recruitment Strategy**

**Key Account Manager—Retail:** This position involves managing key relationships with major retailers such as Tesco and Sainsbury's, negotiating product placement, and developing promotional strategies to ensure maximum in-store exposure of the products. The account manager must work closely with the retailer's buying teams to adapt Beyond Meat's seafood products to meet market demands, ensuring a competitive position on the store shelves.

**Business Development Manager—Food service:** This role would be required to secure new food service accounts and enhance existing relationships, for example, with a company like Pret a Manger. Responsibilities will include pitching to prospective clients, identifying market trends, and working with food service clients on the launch of limited-time menu items or seasonal promotions featuring Beyond Meat's seafood line of products.

**Brand Ambassador:** This role will focus on consumer education and in-store promotions. Brand Ambassadors in high-traffic retail locations educate consumers about the benefits of plant-based seafood and provide samples to create awareness and drive interest.

**Hiring Strategy**

**Channels:** Beyond Meat can use LinkedIn, job boards specific to the industry, and university relationships in their networks that focus on the study of sustainability and business. Specialized recruitment agencies with FMCG and plant-based product experience will also be useful in finding people from relevant backgrounds.

**Selection Criteria:** The company needs individuals who have previously handled FMCG or plant-based food. They also need to be passionate about sustainability. The company will seek an individual with an equal inclination toward communication and negotiation. Knowledge of the seafood or alternative protein market will provide them with cutting-edge account management since such experience will help them negotiate better and strike a chord with clients and consumers.

## Training Requirements

Beyond Meat should ensure bespoke training programs for the new product line. In-house training on specific production processes and health benefits of plant-based seafood will allow the team to answer technical questions and confidently promote the product. Additionally, external training on sustainable food trends can help build further knowledge within the team on what consumers expect of alternatives in seafood. Training will be provided internally through product sessions and externally with courses on industry insights for a well-rounded, knowledgeable team.

### Compensation and Incentives

For this to succeed, Beyond Meat needs to develop a compensation scheme for the sales team so that their base pay is balanced with performance-based incentives as per the job responsibilities. A salary-plus-commission model is most appropriate for key account and business development managers. Offering a competitive base salary, with a commission based on quarterly targets, will ensure financial stability while motivating high performance. For example, bonuses could be tied to meeting specific revenue milestones or growing the number of retail and food service accounts carrying the seafood line.

Since the role involves educating and engaging consumers, brand ambassadors should be remunerated with a fixed base salary with bonuses for achieving specific metrics such as successful in-store activations, consumer engagement level, or promotional conversion rate. All members can be rewarded quarterly bonuses based on attaining or surpassing sales and engagement targets. This structure encourages ongoing motivation rather than focusing solely on end-of-year results.

Beyond Meat can also introduce recognition awards for star performers in the team, such as "Sales Innovator of the Quarter," whereby achievement and team morale are given publicity across boards. Sustainability Incentives: Beyond Meat can thus introduce additional rewards related to sustainability initiatives, such as bonuses for eco-friendly/greens-on promotions within accounts. This would lead better toward the company's mission and value and encourage the sales team to focus on environmentally beneficial activities. The combination of salary, commission, and performance-related bonuses will appeal to experienced professionals who will lead to a motivated and achieving team that complements the goals Beyond Meat has set for business and sustainability.

## Conclusion

The introduction of Beyond Meat's plant-based seafood line in the UK is an excellent opportunity to expand its product and expand into a new line that aligns with trends in sustainability and health. Beyond Meat will ensure this new line of business is well-positioned for success via a dedicated Seafood Sales Team through targeted recruitment, training, and compensation. Strategic partnerships with retail and food service clients and motivated and knowledgeable sales personnel will help Beyond Meat solidify its position as a plant-based innovator, leading brand growth and having a long-term impact in the emerging sustainable foods markets.

# References

Erangu, S., & Mohankumar, P. (2021, January). *(PDF) Is the UK ready for plant-based diets?* ResearchGate.

https://www.researchgate.net/publication/348649311_Is_the_UK_ready_for_plant-based_diets

Impossible. (2024). *Our plant-based ingredients.* Impossible Foods.

https://impossiblefoods.com/nutrition/plant-based-impossible-ingredients

Keith. (2024, September 16). *Beyond Meat PESTLE Analysis - PESTLE ANALYSIS OF COMPANIES AND BRANDS.* PESTLE ANALYSIS of COMPANIES and BRANDS.

https://pestelanalysis.education/beyond-meat-pestle-analysis/

Terazono, E. (2022, February 25). Beyond Meat takes a beating as the plant-based sector reports slowing sales. *Financial Times.* https://www.ft.com/content/9ccf053a-e710-462f-9a8e-1dd0db13a523

The Strategy Story. (2023, August 26). *Beyond Meat PESTEL Analysis.* The Strategy Story.

https://thestrategystory.com/blog/beyond-meat-pestel-analysis/

USDA Foreign Agricultural Service. (2022, January 21). *United Kingdom: Overview of the Plant-Based Food and Beverage Market in the United Kingdom | USDA Foreign Agricultural Service.* Fas.usda.gov. https://fas.usda.gov/data/united-kingdom-overview-plant-based-food-and-beverage-market-united-kingdom

UNCTAD. (2017, February 24). *A Man-made Tragedy: The Overexploitation of Fish Stocks | UNCTAD.* Unctad.org. https://unctad.org/news/man-made-tragedy-overexploitation-fish-stocks